AAT Advanced Diploma in Accounting

Level 3

Final Accounts Preparation

Second edition 2017

ISBN 9781 5097 1242 7

British Library Cataloguing-in-Publication Data

A catalogue record for this book is available from the British Library

Published by

BPP Learning Media Ltd,
BPP House, Aldine Place,
142-144 Uxbridge Road,
London W12 8AA

www.bpp.com/learningmedia

Printed in the United Kingdom

Welcome to BPP Learning Media's AAT **Passcards** for **Final Accounts Preparation**.

- They **save you time**. Important topics are summarised for you.
- They incorporate **diagrams** to kick-start your memory.
- They follow the overall **structure** of the BPP Course Book, but BPP's AAT **Passcards** are not just a condensed book. Each card has been separately designed for clear presentation. Topics are self contained and can be grasped visually.
- AAT **Passcards** are **just the right size** for pockets and bags.
- AAT **Passcards focus on the assessment** you will be facing.
- AAT **Passcards focus on the essential points** that you need to know in the workplace, or when completing your assessment.

Run through the complete set of **Passcards** as often as you can during your final revision period. The day before the assessment, try to go through the **Passcards** again! You will then be well on your way to completing your assessment successfully.

Good luck!

For reference to the Bibliography of the AAT Final Accounts Preparation Passcards please go to: www.bpp.com/learning-media/about/bibliographies

		Page

The BPP **Question Bank** contains activities and assessments that provide invaluable practice in the skills you need to complete this assessment successfully.

Notes

1: Organisations and their final accounts

Topic List

Different types of organisation

Companies Act 2006

Limited liability partnerships (LLPs)

Professional ethics

Threats to independence and conflicts of interest

Data protection and security

There are several different types of organisation, each with its own advantages and disadvantages.

Accountants are bound by a Code of Ethics *which sets out fundamental principles of ethical behaviour.*

Accounting is a way of recording, analysing and summarising the transactions of an entity

There are three main types of profit-making business entity

Sole trader

The sole trader owns his or her own business. They may have employees.

Partnership

Two or more people may go into business together, sharing risks and rewards. Examples are accounting firms, solicitors, dentists.

Limited liability company

Limited liability companies are owned by their shareholders and managed by directors. The company itself is a **separate legal entity**.

Not-for-profit entities

Examples:

- Charities
- Clubs and societies
- Non-governmental organisations (NGOs).

Charities

Regulated nationally eg by Charities Commission in UK.

Charities are regulated by accounting standards, charity law, relevant company law and best practice.

Charities produce:

- A Statement of Financial Position
- A Statement of Financial Activities (SOFA)
- An Annual Report to the Charity Commission
- Sometimes an income and expenditure account.

These are prepared in line with a the Statement of Recommended Practice (SORP).

In other countries, requirements will be different.

Limited liability companies

Limited liability companies offer limited liability to their owners (shareholders). If the company becomes insolvent, the maximum amount that an owner stands to lose is his share of the capital of the business. This is an attractive prospect to investors. Limited liability companies may be private or public. IAS 1 sets out a suggested format for financial statements.

- Owners = shareholders or members
- Large number of owners
- Owner/manager split
- Owners appoint directors to run business on their behalf
- Owners receive share of profits in form of dividends

Disadvantages

- Compliance with national legislation
- Compliance with national accounting standards and/or IASs
- Any formation or annual registration costs

Funding

Companies are funded in the following ways:

- Retained profits
- Short term liabilities (trade payables etc)
- Share capital
- Loan notes

Partnerships

A partnership is an arrangement between two or more individuals in which they undertake to share the risks and rewards of a joint business operation.

The financial arrangements agreed between the partners are often set out in a formal document called a partnership agreement.

If there is no agreement, Partnership Act 1890 applies.

- Profits shared equally
- No salaries or interest on capital
- 5% interest on loans

Advantages of partnership

Partnership v sole trader

- Spread risk
- Network of contacts
- Partners bring in business, skills and experience
- Easier to raise finance

Partnership v limited company

- No need to comply with statutory requirements such as audit
- No need to comply with accounting standards
- No formation or registration fees

 However, note the following **disadvantages**.

- Profits spread
- Dilution of control
- Disputes between partners

- Jointly liable for debts / losses

Companies Act 2006

All UK registered companies must comply with the Companies Act 2006.

The Act's main requirements are:

- The directors must prepare and approve annual accounts and circulate them to the shareholders.
- The accounts must be filed with the Registrar of Companies (ie published).
- Quoted companies must prepare and file IFRS accounts.
- Other companies prepare either:
    - Companies Act accounts (following UK standards); or
    - IFRS accounts (following IFRSs and IASs).
- Directors have a legal duty to keep adequate accounting records.
- Published accounts must show a **true and fair view** (in IAS 1 called **fair presentation**).

Limited liability partnerships (LLPs)

A key disadvantage of partnerships is that the partners have unlimited liability.

LLPs try to solve this problem. The LLP is a separate legal entity, but is run like a partnership, eg the LLP itself pays no tax, with partners (called 'members') being taxed as individuals instead.

LLPs do, however, have more in common with companies than with partnerships:

- They are bound by the Companies Act 2006
- LLPs must file accounts with Companies House

An accountant has five **fundamental ethical principles.**

Integrity	Straightforward, honest, implies fair dealing and truthfulness.
Objectivity	Uncompromised by bias, conflict of interest or the undue influence of others.
Professional competence and due care	Maintain professional knowledge and skill and act diligently.
Confidentiality	Refrain from disclosure of confidential information, and from using such information for personal (or third party) advantage.
Professional behaviour	Comply with relevant laws and regulations, and avoid any action that may bring the profession into disrepute.

The **principles-based approach** to ethics encourages **case-by-case judgement.**

Advantages of 'principles' approach

- Rigorous – comply with the spirit
- 'Bigger picture'
- Flexible for changing circumstances
- Promotes development of skills and judgement
- Creates a culture of ethical awareness
- Encourages personal responsibility

Disdvantages of 'principles' approach

- Not easy to find the right answer
- May be more than one course of action
- Conflicting interests need to be balanced

Advantages of 'rules' approach

- Clear-cut
- Correct course of action will be more obvious
- Easier to enforce

Disdvantages of 'rules' approach

- Loopholes can be found
- 'Tick box' mentality promoted
- Have to legislate for every eventuality
- New requirements must be developed
- Too detailed – miss the 'bigger picture'

Compliance with the fundamental principles may potentially be threatened by a broad range of circumstances:

Threats

- **Self-interest** threat   eg   financial interests, incentive compensation arrangements, undue dependence on fees

- **Self-review** threat   eg   data being reviewed by the same person responsible for preparing it

- **Advocacy** threat   eg   represent an assurance client in litigation or disputes with third parties

- **Familiarity** threat   eg   former partner of the firm being a director or officer of the client

- **Intimidation** threat   eg   threat of dismissal or replacement, being pressured to reduce inappropriately the extent of work performed in order to reduce fees

Data protection and security

The **key risks** affecting data are:

(a) Human error
(b) Technical malfunction
(c) Deliberate/malicious action
(d) Hacking

Accountants should identify and mitigate these risks in order to protect their clients and other stakeholders.

2: Incomplete records

Topic List

Types of error

Sales tax (VAT)

Deriving missing figures from incomplete information

The accounting equation

Goods drawn by proprietor

This area tests your accounts preparation knowledge.

You need to know how the accounts fit together in order to fill in the blanks.

Errors in the trial balance

Type of error	Example
Omission	Both sides of a transaction completely left out.
Original entry	Debits = credits, but amount is incorrect. Eg, a credit sale of £1,000 is posted as: DEBIT Sales ledger control account £150 CREDIT Sales £150
Reversal of entries	Transaction recorded at correct amount, but debit and credit entries have been reversed. Eg, posting the credit sale above as: DEBIT Sales £1,000 CREDIT Sales ledger control account £1,000
Principle	Here debits = credits, but one entry has been made to the wrong type of account. Eg, £500 spent on repairing a motor vehicle has been recorded as: DEBIT Motor vehicles at cost £500 CREDIT Bank £500 Repairs are an item of expense (SOPL), whereas the item has been recorded as a non-current asset (SOFP).

Type of error	Example
Commission	Debits = credits, but entry made to the wrong account, but not the wrong type of account. Eg, £200 spent on telephone costs has been recorded as: DEBIT Insurance expense £200 CREDIT Bank £200 Both accounts (telephone and insurance costs) are expenses, so this is an error of commission rather than of principle.
Entry duplicated on one side, nothing on the other	Here two debit entries or two credit entries have been posted. Eg, the credit sale of £300 above has been posted as: DEBIT Sales ledger control account £300 DEBIT Sales £300 Here debits ≠ credits and so the trial balance will not balance.
Account balance incorrectly transferred to trial balance	Here the final balance on the nominal ledger account is incorrectly transferred to the trial balance. Eg, a balance of £560 on the sales account was recorded in the trial balance as £650 or £400. Here debits ≠ credits and so the trial balance will not balance.

Types of tasks

An incomplete records task may require competence in dealing with one or more of the following:

- Preparation of accounts from information in the task
- Theft of cash (balance on the cash in hand account is unknown)
- Theft or destruction of inventory (closing inventory is the unknown figure)
- Estimated figures, eg 'drawings are between £15 and £20 per week'
- Calculation of capital by means of net assets
- Calculation of profit by P = increase in net assets plus drawings minus increase in capital

VAT revision

- VAT is a sales tax that is charged on most goods/services at standard rate of 20%.
- Output tax is VAT charged on sales.
- Input tax is VAT incurred on purchases/expenses.
- The excess of output tax over input tax is paid over to HM Revenue and Customs (HMRC) quarterly.
- If input tax is more than output tax, HMRC pays the excess back to the business quarterly.
- Prices to customers can be expressed as exclusive or inclusive of VAT.

Credit sales and receivables

The key lies in the formula linking sales, cash receipts and receivables.

Remember:

Opening receivables + sales – cash receipts = closing receivables

Alternatively, put all the workings into a control account to calculate the figure you want.

Sales ledger control account

	£		£
Opening receivables	X	Cash receipts	X
Sales	X	Closing receivables	X
	X		X

Credit purchases and payables

Similarly you need a formula for linking purchases, cash payments and payables.

Opening payables + purchases – cash payments = closing payables

Alternatively, put all the workings into a control account to calculate the figure you want.

Purchases ledger control account

	£		£
Cash payments	X	Opening payables	X
Closing payables	<u>X</u>	Purchases	<u>X</u>
	<u>X</u>		<u>X</u>

Gross margins and mark ups

Other incomplete records problems revolve around the relationship between sales, cost of sales and gross profit: in other words, they are based on reconstructing a trading account.

Gross profit may be expressed either as a percentage of cost of sales or as a percentage of sales.

- Gross profit is 25% of cost of sales (ie 25/100). The terminology is a '25% mark up' (on cost).

		%
	Cost of sales	100
Plus	Gross profit	25
Equals	Sales	125

- Gross profit can also be expressed as 20% of sales. The terminology is a '20% gross margin or gross profit percentage' (on sales).

		%
	Cost of sales	80
Plus	Gross profit	20
Equals	Sales	100

Stolen or destroyed goods

The cost of goods stolen/destroyed can be calculated as follows:

	£
Cost of goods sold based on gross profit margin or mark up	A
Cost of goods sold calculated using standard formula	
(ie opening inventory plus net purchases less closing inventory)	(B)
Difference (lost/stolen goods)	C

- If no goods have been lost, A and B should be the same and therefore C should be nil.
- If goods have been lost, B will be larger than A, because some goods which have been purchased were neither sold nor remaining in inventory, ie they have been lost.

Cash book

Incomplete records problems often concern small retail businesses where sales are mainly for cash. A three-column cash book is often the key to preparing financial statements:

- The bank column records cheques drawn on the business bank account and cheques received from customers and other sources.
- The cash column records till receipts and any expenses or drawings paid out of till receipts before banking.
- The discounts (allowed and received) columns are memoranda only.

Debits (receipts)			Credits (payments)		
Disc all'd	Cash	Bank	Cash	Bank	Disc rec'd
£	£	£	£	£	£

Don't forget that movements between cash and bank need to be recorded by contra entries. This will usually be cash receipts lodged in the bank (debit bank column, credit cash column), but could also be withdrawals of cash from the bank to top up the till (debit cash column, credit bank column).

Again, incomplete records problems will often feature an unknown figure to be derived. Enter in the credit of the cash column all amounts known to have been paid from till receipts: expenses, drawings, lodgements into bank. Enter in the debit of the cash column all receipts from cash customers or other cash sources.

- The balancing figure may then be a large debit, representing the value of **cash sales** if that is the unknown figure.
- Alternatively it may be a credit entry that is needed to balance the cash account, representing the amount of **cash drawings** or of **cash stolen**.

Drawings

Note three tricky points about drawings:

- Owner pays personal money into business bank account

    DEBIT   Bank
    CREDIT   Drawings

- Owner pays personal expenses out of the business bank account or till

    DEBIT   Drawings
    CREDIT   Bank/cash

- Wording of an assessment task

    - 'Drawings approximately £40 per week'
      $\therefore$ drawings for year = £40 $\times$ 52 = £2,080

    - 'Drawings between £35 and £45 per week'
      $\therefore$ drawings are a missing number to be calculated.

Accruals and prepayments

When there is an accrued expense or prepayment, the statement of profit or loss charge can be calculated from the opening balance, the cash movement and the closing balance.

Sometimes it helps to use a 'T' account, as follows in this example for rent.

Rent

	£		£
Prepayment: bal b/d	700	P/L (bal fig)	9,000
Cash	9,300	Prepayment: bal c/d	1,000
	10,000		10,000

3: Accounts for sole traders

Topic List

Financial statements

Cost of goods sold and inventory in the trial balance

You need to be able to prepare the financial statements of a sole trader. Tasks usually require preparation of financial statements from the final trial balance. You must be comfortable with this type of task.

1 Owner and business are not legally separate

BUT

For accounting purposes they are treated as SEPARATE ENTITIES

2 Sole trader takes drawings, not wages, in cash or in kind:

DR Drawings		DR Drawings
CR Cash	OR	CR Purchases

3 Sole trader owns business's NET ASSETS = CAPITAL

Opening capital/net assets	X
Add capital contributed in year	X
Add profit for year	X
Less drawings	(X)
Closing capital/net assets	X

Statement of profit or loss

Income	less	Expenses	equals	Profit/(loss)

Income

Sales revenue   A

Discount received   B

Expenses

Cost of goods sold	
Opening inventory	X
Purchases	X
Closing inventory	(X)
	C

Reduction in expense

Profit/(loss)

Capital in statement of financial position

Expenses	
Electricity	X
Distribution costs	X
Office costs	X
Wages	X
	D

Statement of profit or loss for period

Sales revenue	A
Cost of goods sold	(C)
Gross profit	X
Discount received	B
Expenses	(D)
Profit/(loss)	E/(E)

Statement of financial position

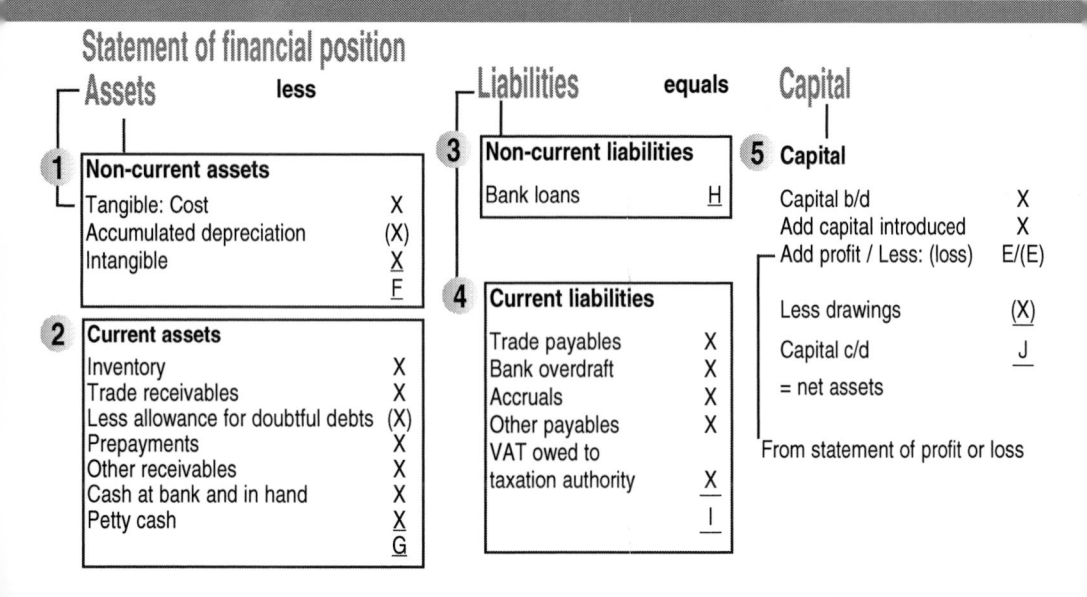

| Assets | less | Liabilities | equals | Capital |

1 Non-current assets

Tangible: Cost	X
Accumulated depreciation	(X)
Intangible	X
	F

2 Current assets

Inventory	X
Trade receivables	X
Less allowance for doubtful debts	(X)
Prepayments	X
Other receivables	X
Cash at bank and in hand	X
Petty cash	X
	G

3 Non-current liabilities

Bank loans	H

4 Current liabilities

Trade payables	X
Bank overdraft	X
Accruals	X
Other payables	X
VAT owed to taxation authority	X
	I

5 Capital

Capital b/d	X
Add capital introduced	X
Add profit / Less: (loss)	E/(E)
Less drawings	(X)
Capital c/d	J
= net assets	

From statement of profit or loss

Statement of financial position as at end of period

1	Non-current assets	F
2	Current assets	G
4	Non-current liabilities	(I)
	Net current assets	X
3	Non-current liabilities	(H)
	Net assets	J
5	Capital	J

Balances brought down on the individual nominal ledger accounts are used to extract an initial or preliminary trial balance. Errors are corrected and adjustments made using an extended trial balance.

Ideally it should be a straightforward matter to use the figures in the final trial balance to draw up the statement of financial position and statement of profit or loss.

However, bear in mind the following points:

- You must know the **format** for an statement of profit or loss and statement of financial position.

- You will need to produce **workings** to get the figures in the trial balance into a suitable format.

Examples of workings

- Sales and sales returns to be netted off
- Cost of sales working
- Carrying amount of all non-current assets for financial statements. Note – total depreciation charge to the statement of profit or loss
- Receivables – need to add in prepayments and take off any allowance
- Payables – need to add in accruals

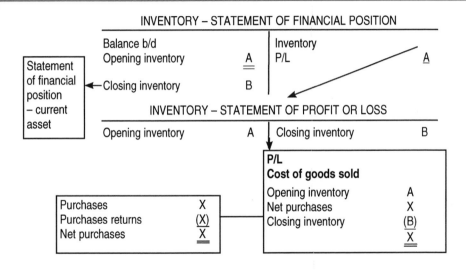

INVENTORY – STATEMENT OF FINANCIAL POSITION

Balance b/d		Inventory	
Opening inventory	A	P/L	A
Closing inventory	B		

Statement of financial position – current asset ← Closing inventory

INVENTORY – STATEMENT OF PROFIT OR LOSS

| Opening inventory | A | Closing inventory | B |

P/L
Cost of goods sold

Opening inventory	A
Net purchases	X
Closing inventory	(B)
	X

Purchases	X
Purchases returns	(X)
Net purchases	X

Notes

4: Accounts for partnerships

Topic List

Partnership accounts have a lot in common with sole trader accounts. However, there are differences in the way profit is appropriated and the way capital is presented in the statement of financial position.

Partnership: an arrangement between two or more individuals which they undertake to share the risks and rewards of a joint business operation.

Partnership agreement

There is usually a partnership agreement setting out the financial arrangements, for example:

- The amount of capital to be provided by each partner

- The division of profits between partners:

  – Salaries

  – Interest on capital

  – Residual profit share (a ratio in which residual profits are to be shared by the partners)

  – Interest charged on drawings

No partnership agreement

Partnership Act 1890 applies.

The statement of profit or loss is the same as a sole trader, but with a partnership the profit needs to be shared out ('appropriated') by the partners.

Statement of profit or loss

Sole trader	£	Partnership	£
Sales	X	Sales	X
Cost of goods sold	(X)	Cost of goods sold	(X)
Gross profit	X	Gross profit	X
Less expenses	(X)	Less expenses	(X)
Profit for period	X	Profit for period	X

All belongs to sole trader

Shared between partners according to the partnership agreement

Profit Appropriation Account

Steps

1. Allocate the partner salaries

2. Allocate any interest on capital

3. Allocate commission earned by partners (eg sales commission)

4. Charge any interest on drawings

5. Allocate remaining profit balance in profit sharing ratio (PSR)

	£
Profit for appropriation	26,000
Salaries:	
Partner A	–4,000
Partner B	–2,500
Partner C	0
Interest on capital:	
Partner A	–400
Partner B	–150
Partner C	–800
Sales commission	
Partner A	–100
Partner B	–50
Partner C	–200

	£
Residual profit available for distribution:	17,800
Share of residual profit or loss:	
Partner A (40%)	7,120
Partner B (20%)	3,560
Partner C (40%)	7,120
Total residual profit or loss distributed	17,800

This means that the total profit of £26,000 is appropriated between the three partners as follows:

- Partner A   £11,620 (£4,000 + £400 + £100 + £7,120)
- Partner B   £6,260 (£2,500 + £150 + 50 + £3,560)
- Partner C   £8,120 (£0 + £800 + £200 + £7,120)

Note. The **profit share** is always the last entry, splitting the residual profit after all other allocations.

Statement of financial position

Sole trader	£	Partnership	£
Proprietor's interest		**Capital accounts**	
Capital	X	Partner A	X
Profit	X	Partner B	X
Less drawings	(X)		X
	X	**Capital accounts**	
		Partner A	X
		Partner B	X
			X
			X

Amount owed back to the **owner** by the business

Amount owed back to the **partners** by the business

4: Accounts for partnerships

Capital accounts

Represent capital invested by each individual partner.

Can be shown as one T account subdivided into columns.

For example:

Capital account

	Partner A £	Partner A £		Partner A £	Partner B £
			Balance b/d	5,000	8,000

Capital accounts

Record each partner's day to day transactions with the business.

The main entries will be: the partners' appropriation of profits (salary, interest on capital and profit share), less drawings and any interest charged on those drawings.

Current account

	Partner A £	Partner A £		Partner A £	Partner B £
Drawings	2,900	970	Balance b/d	1,000	1,500
Interest on drawings	100	30	Salaries	1,500	0
			Interest on capital	500	800
Balance c/d	4,000	5,000	Share of profit or loss	4,000	3,700
	7,000	6,000		7,000	6,000

Admission of a new partner

1 Prepare the statement of profit or loss.

2 Split between pre-change and post-change periods as instructed.

3 Pre-change profit
- Appropriate salary, interest and profit share using **old** partnership agreement.
- Allow an extra column for new partner, in both current and capital accounts.

4 Credit goodwill (given in task) to **old** partners in old PSR in their capital accounts.

5 Eliminate the goodwill by debiting all the partners (ie **include the newly admitted partner**) in the **new** PSR.

6 Balance off the capital accounts.

7 Post-change profit
  - Appropriate remainder of profit using **new** partnership agreement re salary, interest and profit share.

8 Put drawings through the current accounts.

9 Prepare the statement of financial position if required to do so.

Retirement of a partner

1 Prepare the statement of profit or loss.

2 Split profit between pre-change and post-change periods, on the basis indicated in the task (eg three months pre-change, nine months post-change).

3 Pre-change profit
- Appropriate salary, interest and profit share using **old** partnership agreement and profit share.
- Put old partner's drawings through current account.

4 Balance off retiring partner's **current** account **only**, and transfer the balance to their **capital** account.

5
- Credit **old** partners in **old PSR** in their capital accounts with goodwill (given in task).
- This will provide the retiring partner with an increase in the partnership's worth that has arisen while they were a partner.

6 Calculate retiring partner's final capital balance and remove it – the task will give instructions, eg:

- Pay in cash (DR capital a/c; CR cash)
- Create a loan account (DR capital a/c; CR loan)

7 Eliminate the goodwill by debiting all the remaining partners in the **new** PSR with the goodwill amount.

8 Balance off the capital accounts.

9 Post-change profit

- Appropriate using **new** partnership agreement re salary, interest and profit share.

10 Prepare the statement of financial position if required to do so (don't forget the loan accounts, if any).

Changes to the partnership – goodwill

When a partner retires from the partnership or a new partner is admitted to the partnership, it is usual for the partners to value the business. The worth of a business over and above its individual net assets is called **goodwill**.

	£
Property	200,000
Other assets	120,000
	320,000
Liabilities	(100,000)
	220,000

This business therefore has a '**book value**' of £220,000.

However, when the partnership was valued as a whole, it was judged to be worth £350,000. Therefore, there is a difference of £130,000 above book value.

- £80,000 of this difference was believed to be attributable to an increase in the value of the property.

- The other £50,000 was due to the business's superb regional reputation and wealthy customer base.

- This £50,000 is known as goodwill.

Goodwill is first added to the partners' **capital** accounts according to the existing or **old PSR**.

Account name	Debit £	Credit £
Goodwill	X	
Capital account (using existing PSR)		X

Goodwill is an extremely subjective figure and so it is **not** left in the partnership's statement of financial position, but is removed.

This is done using the **new PSR**.

Account name	Debit £	Credit £
Capital accounts (using new PSR)	X	
Goodwill		X

Notes

5: Introduction to limited company accounts

Topic List

The regulatory framework

Generally accepted accounting practice (GAAP)

Accounting standards

Conceptual Framework

IFRS financial statements

Notes to the financial statements

IAS 16 and IAS 2

Elements of the financial statements

There are several important ways in which a limited company differs from a sole trader or a partnership.

Limited companies are required to observe various rules and regulations when preparing financial statements.

Accounting regulations aim to ensure that financial statements actually do provide useful information:

- They promote comparability between different entities and over time, by ensuring that accounts are prepared in line with a common set of standards.

- By requiring accounts to be prepared in line with objective standards, management is prevented from simply presenting information about the company in the best possible light.

- Accounting regulations help ensure that the information in the accounts is relevant to the people who use them, eg the owners of the company (its shareholders).

Generally accepted accounting practice (GAAP)

GAAP refers to established national accounting procedures, but is not defined precisely.

GAAP is normally made up of:

- Accounting standards (eg IFRS)
- National company law (eg Companies Act 2006 in the UK)
- Stock exchange requirements (for companies quoted on a recognised stock exchange)

Accounting standards

- Authoritative statements of how particular types of transactions and other events should be reflected in financial statements.

- Fair presentation/true and fair view = compliance with accounting standards.

Two sets of accounting standards:

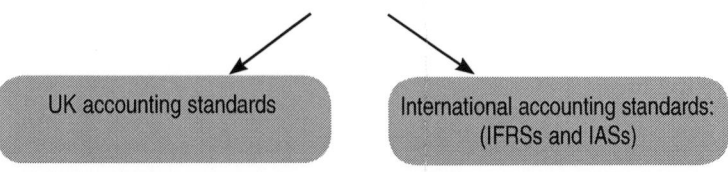

UK accounting standards

International accounting standards: (IFRSs and IASs)

In your Assessment, you will be expected to prepare financial statements that comply with **International Financial Reporting Standards**.

International Financial Reporting Standards

Since January 2005, all EU quoted companies, including UK companies, have been required to use international financial reporting standards. Two types are in force:

- International Financial Reporting Standards (IFRSs): issued by the International Accounting Standards Board (IASB) since 2001.
- International Accounting Standards (IASs): issued before 2001 by the IASB's predecessor, the International Accounting Standards Committee (IASC).

'Principles -based' approach

IFRSs take a 'principles-based' approach, rather than a 'rules-based' approach. Each IFRS sets out general principles which should be applied, instead of giving a list of detailed rules to comply with.

The purpose of financial statements

The purpose of financial statements is to provide information about an organisation's:

- Financial position (assets and liabilities)
- Financial performance (profit or loss)
- Changes in financial position (cash flows)

The IASB's *Conceptual Framework*

The *Conceptual Framework* sets out the principles and concepts that the IASB believes should underlie the preparation and presentation of financial statements.

It is not an accounting standard.

Objective of financial statements (general purpose financial reporting)

To provide financial information about the reporting entity that is useful to existing and potential investors, lenders and other creditors in making decisions about providing resources to the entity.

Going concern

Financial statements are prepared on the assumption that the entity will continue to operate for the foreseeable future; no intention to liquidate or curtail scale of operations materially.

Accruals

Under the accruals concept the effects of transactions and other events are **recognised when they occur**.

This means that:

- Income and expenses are recorded in the financial statements when entity has **earned the income / incurred the cost**, not when cash is received or paid.
- Income and costs are matched to each other, so the cost of buying something that a business later sells is shown in the same financial period as the income from the sale.
- Items are reported in the financial statements of the period to which they relate.

Qualitative characteristics of useful financial information

Fundamental qualitative characteristics

Useful information:

- Is **relevant**: it is capable of making a difference in decisions (includes **materiality**).
- **Faithfully represents** what it purports to represent: it is complete, neutral and free from error.

Enhancing qualitative characteristics

These characteristics enhance the usefulness of information that is relevant and faithfully represented.

- Comparability
- Verifiability

- Timeliness
- Understandability

Presentation of Financial Statements (IAS 1)

IAS 1 (para. 36) states that a complete set of financial statements should be prepared at least annually.

A complete set of financial statements comprises:

- A statement of financial position
- A statement of profit or loss and other comprehensive income
- A statement of changes in equity
- A statement of cash flows
- Notes

Proforma – statement of profit or loss

XYZ Ltd

Statement of profit or loss for the year ended 31 December 20X2

	20X2 £000	20X1 £000
Revenue	X	X
Cost of sales	(X)	(X)
Gross profit	X	X
Distribution costs	(X)	(X)
Administrative expenses	(X)	(X)
Profit from operations	X	X
Finance costs	(X)	(X)
Profit before tax	X	X
Tax	(X)	(X)
Profit for the year	X	X

Proforma – statement of financial position

A statement of financial position shows the assets, liabilities and equity of a business at a stated date.

XYZ Ltd

Statement of financial position as at 31 December 20X2

	20X2 £000	20X1 £000
ASSETS		
Non-current assets		
Intangible assets	X	X
Property, plant and equipment	X	X
	X	X
Current assets		
Inventories	X	X
Trade and other receivables	X	X
Cash and cash equivalents	X	X
	X	X
Total assets	X	X

	20X2 £000	20X1 £000
EQUITY AND LIABILITIES		
Equity		
Share capital	X	X
Share premium	X	X
Retained earnings	X	X
Revaluation surplus	X	X
Total equity	X	X
Non-current liabilities		
Bank loans	X	X
	X	X
Current liabilities		
Trade and other payables	X	X
Short-term borrowings	X	X
Tax liability	X	X
	X	X
Total liabilities	X	X
Total equity and liabilities	X	X

Notes to the financial statements

Notes are provided:

- Where it is required by other IFRSs
- Where additional information is needed

Typically, many of the notes provide further analysis of the totals shown in the main financial statements, eg of property, plant and equipment, of inventories, or of trade receivables and payables.

Accounting policies

The notes to the financial statements must disclose the accounting policies adopted by the directors of the company.

Companies should select accounting policies which give a 'true and fair view' of their financial performance and position.

Companies are not allowed to change an established accounting policy without good reason.

Property, Plant and Equipment (IAS 16)

Property, plant and equipment are tangible items that:

- Are held for use in the production or supply of goods or services, for rental to others, or for administrative purposes; and
- Are expected to be used during more than one period.

(IAS 16: para. 6)

'Tangible' means that the item has physical substance.

Inventories (IAS 2)

Inventories include raw materials, work-in-progress and finished goods.

The basic rule per IAS 2 Inventories is:

'Inventories should be measured at the **lower of cost and net realisable value**.'

(IAS 2: para. 9)

This is important as overstatement of the value of inventories will lead to overstatement of the company's profits.

The elements of financial statements

- **Asset**: a resource controlled by the entity as a result of past events and from which future economic benefits are expected to flow to the entity.
- **Liability**: a present obligation of the entity arising from past events, the settlement of which is expected to result in an outflow of resources embodying economic benefits from the entity.
- **Equity**: the owners' residual interest in the assets of the entity after deducting all its liabilities.
- **Income**: increases in economic benefits during the accounting period in the form of inflows or enhancement of assets or decreases of liabilities that result in increases in equity, other than those relating to contributions from owners.
- **Expenses**: decreases in economic benefits during the accounting period in the form of outflows or depletions of assets or incurrences of liabilities that result in decreases in equity, other than those relating to distributions to owners.
- **Contributions from owners**: increases in equity resulting from transfers from owners in their capacity as owners (eg issues of share capital).
- **Distributions to owners**: decreases in equity resulting from transfers to owners in their capacity as owners (eg dividends).

The elements and the accounting equation

ASSETS – LIABILITIES = EQUITY

EQUITY = CONTRIBUTIONS FROM OWNERS + INCOME – EXPENSES – DISTRIBUTIONS TO OWNERS

Recognising the elements of financial statements

An item that meets the definition of an element (eg an asset or a liability) should be recognised if:

- It is probable that any future economic benefit associated with the item will flow to or from the entity; and
- The item has a cost or value that can be measured with reliability.

Recognition and the accounting equation

- If net assets increase, income or a gain is recognised; and
- If net assets are reduced or eliminated, an expense or a loss is recognised.

  CLOSING NET ASSETS – OPENING NET ASSETS = PROFIT/LOSS FOR THE PERIOD

Notes

Notes

Notes